Heroes for Young Readers

Written by Renee Taft Meloche

Illustrated by Bryan Pollard

Heroes of History for Young Readers

Written by Renee Taft Meloche

Illustrated by Bryan Pollard

Heroes for Young Readers Activity Guides and audio CDs are also available. See the back of this book for more information.

HEROES FOR YOUNG READERS

DOCTORS KLAUS-DIETER AND MARTINA JOHN

Miracle in Peru

Written by Renee Taft Meloche
Illustrated by Bryan Pollard

Doctors Klaus-Dieter and Martina John: Miracle in Peru   Text © 2018 by Renee Taft Meloche   Illustrations © 2018 by Bryan Pollard
Published by YWAM Publishing, P.O. Box 55787, Seattle, WA 98155   ISBN 978-1-57658-9885   Printed in China.   All rights reserved.

A German teen named Klaus just loved
    to be around one girl,
who had the bluest eyes he'd seen
    and lovely long brown curls.

This girl, Martina, made him smile
    when once he heard her say,
"I'm going to be a doctor for
    the very poor one day."

And that is just exactly what
    Klaus also planned to be:
a doctor who would help the poor
    and care for them for free.

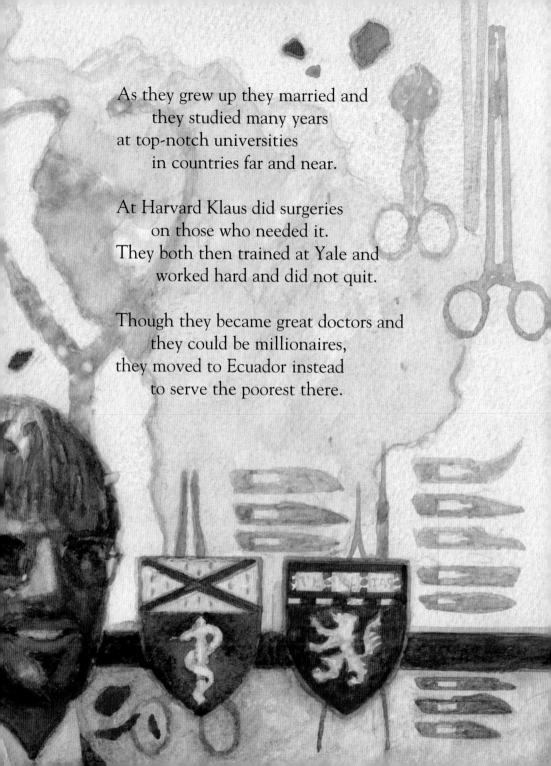

As they grew up they married and
  they studied many years
at top-notch universities
  in countries far and near.

At Harvard Klaus did surgeries
  on those who needed it.
They both then trained at Yale and
  worked hard and did not quit.

Though they became great doctors and
  they could be millionaires,
they moved to Ecuador instead
  to serve the poorest there.

A jungle girl named Andri had
    been bitten by a snake,
so Doctor Klaus knew he must act
    and try to operate.

He prayed, *God help me save her leg.*
    It's something she can't lose!
Her jungle life will be too hard
    with just one leg to use.

So carefully he cut right through
    her red and swollen skin,
then took out all the tissue where
    the poison had gone in.

He operated on the girl,
    not once but seven times,
and this made Andri happy since
    she soon could run and climb.

Now Doctor Tina helped treat kids
        with scrapes and burns and worms,
or who'd been bitten by some bug
        that carried deadly germs.

She also cared for their two kids,
        a little girl and boy,
and then she had another son,
        which brought them further joy.

Now one day Doctor Klaus rode up
        a rocky mountainside
to meet two hundred Indians from
        a poor and peaceful tribe.

These Indian farmers fought high winds
        and heavy rains and storms.
They had no running water and
        no heat to keep them warm.

They once were mighty Incas with
    grand temples made of stone,
until the Spanish army came
    and they were overthrown.

So now instead of large stone walls,
    clay bricks made up each house,
and yet these Indians gladly shared
    their food with Doctor Klaus.

He asked these people, "When you're sick,
    where do you go for care?"
and one replied, "There is no help
    for us from anywhere.
No hospital will let us in
    because we cannot pay."
Then Doctor Klaus thought, *This is wrong.*
    I must help out some way.

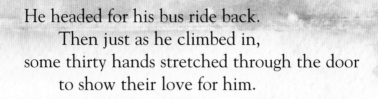

He headed for his bus ride back.
    Then just as he climbed in,
some thirty hands stretched through the door
    to show their love for him.

It also was a plea for help,
    a silent heartfelt cry.
For weeks he saw those outstretched hands
    and knew the reason why.

He loved these mountain Indians and
    he knew what must be done:
he had to build a hospital
    where they could freely come.

Back home in Germany where he
    and Tina used to live,
they shared the Indians' need in hopes
    that some would want to give.

Yet when they talked about their dream,
    some tried to set them straight.
"A hospital? For Indians?
    The costs are much too great!
And what is all this talk of God?
    That's something you can't do.
Most people will not like that and
    won't give a cent to you!"

Yet Doctors Klaus and Tina both
    believed without a doubt
their dream would be impossible
    if God did not help out.

They spoke at churches and at clubs,
    to crowds or just a few.
They shared their dream on radio
    and television too.

They also prayed to God to make
    this hospital come true:
a dream to build near Indians in
    the mountains of Peru.

Some people gave so they could buy
        a good-sized plot of land,
so with their three young kids they flew
        into Peru as planned.

By truck they traveled twenty hours
        to one small Indian town.
The town was in a valley with
        huge mountains all around.

They bought a home where there were cracked
        old window panes and doors.
Some boxes became furniture
        on stained and rotten floors.

The family slept in sleeping bags,
        but what they did not like
was waking up to ants and bugs
        that covered them with bites.

The ceilings were too low for them
        and termites ate through stairs,
but over time they fixed their home
        and really made it theirs.

A famous Inca city built
     high up a mountain ridge
was just a two-day hike from there
     across a narrow bridge.

This place called Machu Picchu, with
     its great stone walls all through,
is famous as an ancient site
     which millions travel to.

As Doctor Klaus kept traveling
    and spoke to all he could,
more people gave and with God's help
    a hospital soon stood.

Four thousand Indians sat for hours
    beneath the midday sun
to celebrate its opening:
    the sick were free to come!

Diospi Suyana was
    the hospital's new name.
These words, which mean "We trust in God,"
    were seen by all who came.

The sick would often walk for hours
    on bruised and blistered feet
to make it to the hospital
    through storms or summer heat.

Soon Doctor Tina started up
        a club where kids could meet.
She taught them Bible stories, crafts,
        and sometimes fed them treats.

Now at the children's club one day,
        a girl named Emily
had red sores on her face that she
        was scared the kids might see.

Some sores had turned to blisters that
        were bigger than a coin.
When other children went to play,
        she did not want to join.

Instead she took her coat and pulled
        it right up to her chin,
but Doctor Tina saw her sores
        and crusty, pussy skin.

She knelt down by the little girl
        and said, "Please come with me,"
and Emily then took her hand
        and followed willingly.

When they got to the hospital—
　　a big but friendly place—
kind Doctor Tina said, "I have
　　a way to treat your face."

She gave a pill to Emily
　　to help to heal her sores.
The next week at the children's club,
　　she checked on her once more.

She saw a happy Emily
　　who grinned from ear to ear.
Her sores and scabs were almost gone.
　　Her skin was soft and clear!

Another little girl named Rose
    was only five years old.
Her hut was dark and windowless
    to help keep out the cold.

One afternoon her mother left
    and she was all alone
to watch her baby brother in
    their small and dreary home.

Rose wore some tiny sandals made
    from worn-out rubber tires.
Because the family had no stove,
    they used an open fire.

Rose wore a hooded sweater and
    as flames grew in the dark,
she sat too near the open fire
    as it began to spark.

Her hooded sweater caught on fire,
    and soon her back was burned!
She fell down on the floor and cried
    until her mom returned.

When Rose got to the hospital,
    her back and neck looked bad.
A surgeon set to work to clean
    the painful burns she had.

He dressed her wounds with bandages,
    and though she was quite shy,
the nurses made her feel at home
    whenever they stopped by.

They gave Rose colored pens and books.
    They sat with her and read.
She drew bright pictures with her pens
    while she remained in bed.

But what made Rose most happy was
    when Doctor Tina came.
Together they would talk a lot
    and play a fun-filled game.

When Rose's many burns had healed,
    her stay came to an end,
yet Doctor Tina checked on her
    and still remained her friend.

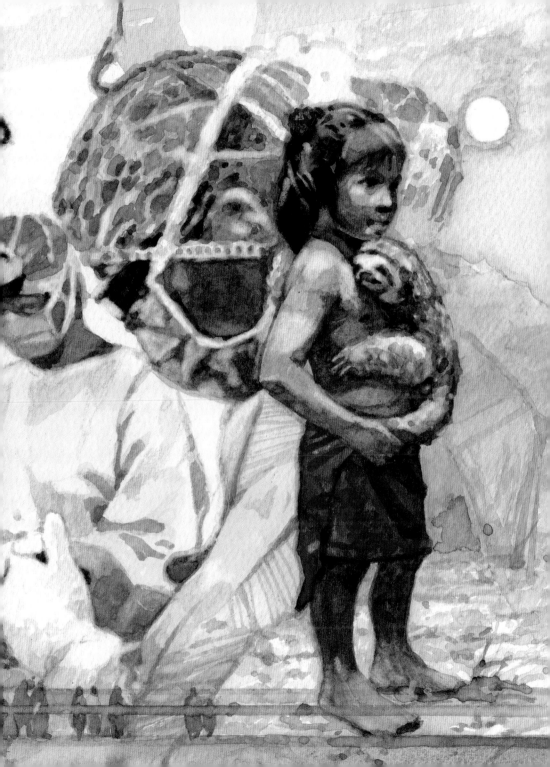

The hospital's equipment and
  its doctors were so good
if you or I got sick, that's where
  we'd all go if we could.

One teenager they tried to help
  was called Geronimo.
He sat alone inside a room
  with no place he could go.

He scooted on the floor since he
  could not walk anymore.
He could not play outside with friends
  or climb trees and explore.

His bones were thin and brittle and
 he hurt from head to toe.
His body was not working right,
 which made it hard to grow.

He had what's called arthritis—
 a terrible disease.
His hips did not move like they should.
 He could not move his knees.

He never learned to read or write,
 though he was very smart.
He used his small weak hands to draw
 and loved creating art.

When Doctor Tina heard about
 Geronimo one day,
she went to visit him to see
 if she could help some way.

She saw him huddled on the floor.
 She checked his heart and lungs,
then took him to the hospital
 to see what could be done.

It was too late to operate.
 His bones were stuck like glue,
and so she gave him medicine,
 which helped the pain he knew.

To make it easier for him
    to get around a bit,
a special wheelchair was found.
    It was a perfect fit.

A teacher came to teach him how
    to read and how to write.
Geronimo learned easily
    because he was so bright.

And at the hospital his art
    of horses, hens, and sheep
was shown to many visitors
    and some bought them to keep.

Since Doctors Klaus and Tina felt
    their home was now Peru,
they soon became proud citizens
    of that grand country too.

Now Indians come from near and far—
    young children, women, men—
to reach the hospital they know
    was built there just for them.

A line goes down and down the road,
    which often starts at night,
so they can be among the first
    to get in once its light.

Though many people thought this dream
    was just a fairy tale,
both Doctors Klaus and Tina knew
    with God they would not fail.

Heroes for Young Readers and Heroes of History for Young Readers are based on the
Christian Heroes: Then & Now and Heroes of History biographies by Janet & Geoff
Benge. Don't miss out on these exciting, true adventures for ages 10 and up!

Christian Heroes: Then & Now
by Janet & Geoff Benge

10183399

Meloche, Renee Taft.
Doctors Klaus-Dieter and
Martina John : miracle in
Peru

:atest Wonder in Egypt
Into All the World
; Her All for China
vard into Calabar
.......u Caviv. Through the Jade Gate
Nate Saint: On a Wing and a Prayer
Paul Brand: Helping Hands
Rachel Saint: A Star in the Jungle
Richard Wurmbrand: Love Your Enemies
Rowland Bingham: Into Africa's Interior
Samuel Zwemer: The Burden of Arabia
Sundar Singh: Footprints Over the Mountains
Wilfred Grenfell: Fisher of Men
William Booth: Soup, Soap, and Salvation
William Carey: Obliged to Go

Heroes of History
by Janet & Geoff Benge

Abraham Lincoln: A New Birth of Freedom
Alan Shepard: Higher and Faster
Ben Carson: A Chance at Life
Benjamin Franklin: Live Wire
Benjamin Rush: The Common Good
Billy Graham: America's Pastor
Captain John Smith: A Foothold in the New World
Christopher Columbus: Across the Ocean Sea
Clara Barton: Courage under Fire
Daniel Boone: Frontiersman
Davy Crockett: Ever Westward
Douglas MacArthur: What Greater Honor
Elizabeth Fry: Angel of Newgate
Ernest Shackleton: Going South
George Washington: True Patriot
George Washington Carver: From Slave to Scientist
Harriet Tubman: Freedombound
John Adams: Independence Forever
Laura Ingalls Wilder: A Storybook Life
Louis Zamperini: Redemption
Meriwether Lewis: Off the Edge of the Map